The
Relaxed
Home School:

A
Family
Production

Also by Mary Hood:

The Home-Schooling Resource Guide
    & Directory of Organizations

Countdown to Consistency

How to Set Up Learning Centers
    in Your Home

Teaching Children to Use
    the Library

The

Relaxed

Home School:

A Family Production

Mary Hood, Ph.D.

Cover Designed and Illustrated by

Laura Hood

Ambleside Educational Press

The Relaxed Home School

Published by Ambleside Educational Press
140 Bond St., Westminster, MD 21157

Cover art by Laura Hood

Printed in the U.S.A.
First printing.

Printed on acid-free paper. ∞

ISBN 0-9639740-0-9

To

Charlotte Mason

who taught me

to

respect

my children

Table of Contents

Introduction   1

The Production Crew   5

Writing The Script   11

Setting the Stage   23

Act I: Natural Literacy   39

Act II: A Living Curriculum   61

On to Broadway!   83

Answering the Critics   95

Postscript: No O.B.E. for me! 105

Introduction

Originally, the picture on the cover of this book was going to be a home-schooling mother lounging in a hammock, sipping a glass of something cool and refreshing. Admittedly, this was not very realistic. Few home-schooling families own hammocks and the mothers would never have the time to use them if they did. Yet something about the image appealed to me ... wishful thinking, perhaps?

While I was making a tentative outline, my thirteen-year-old daughter leaned over and noticed that one of the chapters was going to be called, "Setting the Stage," and another mentioned the mother's "role." She immediately started brainstorming, revising chapter titles, and drawing alternate covers. The rest, as they say, is history.

The drama theme suited my daughter perfectly. She loves working on a stage. When I was younger, I also enjoyed acting, and tried, in a lukewarm fashion, to get my husband interested in musical theatre. It seemed hopeless. He absolutely hated it. Later, when Ginny caught the theatre bug, her intense enthusiasm sparked his flame. Now he knows every Broadway song by heart.

These episodes demonstrate the cooperative atmosphere for work and learning that is the hallmark of a relaxed home school environment. There are no rigid lesson plans in the Hood household anymore. When we started out, back in 1983, I had an armload of textbooks and workbooks for each student. As a "professional," with many preconceived notions about education, it took awhile for me to see the light. Eventually however, the children managed to remind me what real learning was all about, and to show me the folly of most of my carefully prepared plans. Gradually, bit by bit, we have thrown off all the trappings of the institutional school, and have purchased fewer texts and "curriculum materials" each year.

During this time I have had the privilege of meeting and working with hundreds of home-schooling families, through involvement with support groups and my work as an educational consultant. Some of these families have taught me important lessons. Others have gone to extremes, either possessing so much structure that they looked like miniature schools, or so little that they bordered on chaos.

In this book, I'm going to suggest a third approach. A "Relaxed Home School" begins with a definite framework. The parents have thought through their ideas about education carefully and have come to terms with their relationships and roles as parents, allies, and co-educators. They respect their children and welcome their input, whether making or executing plans. They have set some specific overall goals for their family, and their expectations reflect their understanding of individual differences. They have set up a pleasant environment for living and learning together, and have implemented a basic schedule that works well for their family. Within this general framework, however, they have placed a supreme emphasis on the need for flexibility, balance, and mutual respect.

If the ideas in this book sound helpful to you, feel free to use them. Whatever you do, though, don't copy them just because you think that I'm an "expert." If they don't feel right to you, try something else. Always remember: You know your children best! *You* are the expert! Take control of your children's education! And then...

RELAX!!

Chapter I
The Production Crew

It is almost time for the final performance of "The Music Man" to begin. My older children are flying around the house, feverishly applying make-up and reciting lines. Soon it will all be over. The endless costume-fittings, the late-night rehearsals, the opening night jitters and the cast parties will all fade into the past. Only the scrapbooks and the memories will remain.

One week ago, however, nobody was sure the play would even open! The fate of the production hung in the balance when the producer was suddenly carted off to the hospital! Luckily, he had delegated his responsibilities wisely. The backstage crew, the ushers, the chorus members, and the stars all knew their parts well and were able to go on as scheduled. The director, who was given authority and autonomy from the start, experienced few difficulties pulling the production together and carrying on.

A production crew and a home-schooling family have a lot in common. In both cases, the individuals must understand their own roles and work together cooperatively in order to put on a successful performance. In most households, this means that the father takes on the role of the "producer," and the mother is the director.

A theatrical producer bears the ultimate responsibility for establishing the underlying framework, selecting personnel, and handing out work assignments at the start of a play. However, once he has appointed a director, he usually encourages her to assume complete responsibility for that area of the production. The director is considered a "professional" and is given authority and respect by the other team members.

As the "producer" of the home school, the father generally has ultimate responsibility for the family. He is the one who makes sure that the underlying framework is sound, and that all of the family members are living up to their share of the responsibilities. However, because few fathers are around during the day when much of the home-schooling activity takes place, he is not usually the one who has primary responsibility for the day-to-day functioning of the home school. If that is the case, he must be willing to delegate the authority for that job to his "director" or the performance will be jeopardized.

Over the years I have met mothers who had to phone their husbands to get permission to go on spur-of-the moment outings to the zoo or the museum. Some mothers haven't been able to schedule late night programs because their husbands would not grant them the flexibility to sleep late. Other mothers have not been able to go to seminars or curriculum fairs because their husbands felt that they should stay home on the weekends. Still others have attended these functions, but have hesitated to buy needed curriculum materials because they didn't know if they had enough money in the bank.

As "professionals," these mothers *must* have the authority to make these decisions on their own. They need to understand budget constraints and have a certain amount of money set aside to use at their discretion for school-related items. Their attendance at "professional functions," such as curriculum fairs, must be assigned the same degree of importance as their husbands' conferences at work. Without possessing this degree of respect and authority, they can never hope to exercise the control that is needed in the home-school situation.

Most parents originally become home schoolers because they want to be the directing force behind their children's educations. Unfortunately, the first thing many of them do is to give their control away again. Some hand it over to curriculum suppliers or correspondence schools. Others defer to educational supervisors, evaluators, or "home-schooling experts," who claim to know what is right for their individual families. Still others believe so strongly in the rights of children that they never make a serious attempt to establish or exercise parental control in the first place.

When parents relinquish control to "experts," they defeat their original purpose, and might as well return to the institutional setting. When they relinquish control to their children, the result is usually chaos. No matter how much parents believe in democracy within the family, every organization needs to have some kind of authority structure. Without a captain and navigator, a ship at sea will wander aimlessly and founder beneath the waves. Without a producer and a director, the best cast cannot put together a cohesive play. Without caring adults assuming proper leadership roles within a family, the children will be swamped with responsibility before they are mature enough to handle the situation.

In Conclusion

As a home-schooling parent, you begin to gain control when you start the process of thinking through your own beliefs about education carefully. To do this, you need to remember your own experiences with learning, both inside and outside of school. You must analyze the reasons why some learning experiences have remained with you, while others were quickly forgotten. You need to come to terms with your feelings about testing and evaluation, and decide whether or not you want to use a grading system. Even more important, you must establish some basic long-range goals for your family and your individual children. Thinking through these issues will give you a head start towards developing your "educational philosophy," which is an important step in discovering the best methods and materials to use with your particular family.

Chapter II
Writing The Script

Every drama production begins with a written script. The players start by learning the plot, familiarizing themselves with their characters, and memorizing their lines. At some point, most directors will allow the actors to give their own input, and improvise in order to improve the action. However, there has to be a basic script in place before rehearsals begin or people will have no idea how they should proceed.

The corollary to a "script" in a home school setting is a written statement of purpose, or "philosophy of education." This purpose statement should include your basic beliefs about education, a list of goals for your family, and the types of methods and materials you plan to use. At the beginning, it may seem difficult and time-consuming to pull such a plan together, but in the long run it will save a great deal of time.

Why is it so important for you to develop your own philosophy of education? There are several reasons. First, as soon as you really understand where you are going and what you believe about learning, you will find that you can eliminate many unnecessary activities. Those you do plan will be more productive. You will waste less money on curriculum materials that wind up sitting on a shelf. Your approach to education will become more consistent, and you will be equipped to defend that approach to others. Finally, when you know more about educational philosophy, it will help you to recognize and understand alternate points of view, and "sift the wheat from the chaff" when deciding whether to listen to the advice of others.

In this book, for example, I'm going to be presenting my own ideas about education. By the end of the book, if you feel your own philosophy differs from mine, and you don't want to believe anything I say, that's perfectly okay with me! As long as you can articulate your own ideas, and explain why you object to mine, I'll know that you have taken control of your own home-schooling efforts, and that is the important thing!

There are at least four recognizable educational philosophies that have influenced the modern home-schooling movement: essentialism, perennialism, progressivism, and existentialism. These philosophies have been explained in detail in another book I've written, called ***Countdown to Consistency***. Of course, there are really as many educational philosophies as there are people engaging in educational activities. If you have already read ***Countdown to Consistency***, or have gone to the corresponding workshop, I hope you haven't been labeling everyone around you! Most of us don't fit neatly into any particular category. We have adopted what are known as "eclectic" philosophies, taking the best from everything, and developing unique approaches that suit our individual families.

Actually, you already possess your own philosophy of education, whether you realize it or not! You have many ideas about learning which have been developed over the years through your own experiences, both in and out of school. If you will take a little time to clarify these ideas, consider where they came from, and decide if they are still relevant in the home school setting, it will help you immensely in the process of curriculum planning. Because many of your past experiences took place in an institutional school, you may discover that some of the methods you have been planning to use will no longer work in a home school environment.

Your World View

In thinking through your educational philosophy, the first thing you must consider is your overall "world view." This refers to your underlying spiritual or philosophical beliefs about the world around you. My own educational practices are, in many ways, a direct outgrowth of my Christian faith. However, there are other Christians who do things very differently than I do when it comes to education. One of my favorite Bible verses is John 15:5, which likens a belief in Jesus to a tree with a deep root system and a variety of branches. My peace and understanding, as well as my educational beliefs and practices, are all rooted in my relationship with Jesus. However, my particular "branch" of the tree may look very different than my neighbor's, who may share my ultimate belief system but not my way of working with children! This doesn't mean that either of us is necessarily "wrong." After all, God built tremendous diversity into this world. He made every single snowflake with a different crystalline pattern and gave each zebra its own set of stripes, which will never be duplicated anywhere on this earth. Wouldn't it seem capricious if He suddenly changed character and expected all home-schooling families to set aside their unique characteristics and talents and become mere clones of each other?

On the flip side of the coin, there are people of widely divergent religious beliefs who often discover a great deal of common ground when it comes to their educational beliefs. Unfortunately, many people have confused these two issues, and have started arguments that have confused parents and caused needless rifts within the home-schooling movement.

Ideas About Learning

After considering your spiritual or philosophical base, you need to think through your basic ideas about learning. Have you ever stopped to consider how "real learning" takes place? Do you think that it occurs as a result of a teacher standing at the front of the room and lecturing? If a student "learns" something and can spit it out on a test, but forgets it two weeks later, do you honestly believe any true learning has taken place?

Personally, I have observed too many college students while they were studying for exams and scrabbling for grades to believe that the processes of lecturing, testing, and ranking them are anything but counterproductive. I have also been in every position on the grading curve myself and know firsthand the negative effects grades can have on an individual's motivation level and feeling of self-worth.

Many people who believe that tests and grades are effective motivating devices have difficulty understanding how our home school can operate without them. However, I believe that grades are only short-term motivators, and any knowledge gained for the purpose of a test is quickly forgotten. In order for long-range learning to take place, there are only three ways that students can ever be truly motivated.

The first happens when a person is internally motivated to learn something. The child who is in love with dinosaurs will eagerly gobble up any information on the subject and will remember that information years later. That's why "Calvin," the comic strip character, knows so much about prehistoric creatures and does so poorly with the rest of his schoolwork!

The second form of motivation occurs when someone else has an intense love of a subject and transfers their enthusiasm to the student. Most of you probably had a "favorite teacher" who made a particular subject come alive for you. That's also what happened when my husband finally decided to learn something about musical theatre from my daughter when he couldn't (or wouldn't) learn about it from me. My own enthusiasm level just wasn't high enough for it to transfer to someone else!

The final form of motivation comes when people set goals that have personal significance to them, and are willing to do things that are difficult or boring in order to reach them. This form of motivation cannot be transferred through coercion! If a goal is set by parents or teachers, but is never internalized by students, little long-range learning will take place, no matter how many "A's" might be collected along the way.

Goals

Lately, there has been a lot of talk about the establishment of proper educational "goals." The national "Education 2000" plan, coupled with the discussion of "outcomes-based education" that has dominated the news in many areas, have both focused attention on this aspect of education.

I've always believed in setting goals. In fact, I have little lists on scraps of paper all over the house: long-range, medium-range, and short-range goals, goals for the family, the individual children, and my own business. Without them, I don't believe we would function nearly as effectively or make any observable progress towards the things that matter to us. However, the "outcomes-based education" people have a few things backwards. For one thing, they are attempting to set goals that should properly be set by the individual students or their families. Also, the policy makers are delving into the all-important area of values, and they are doing it with the mind-set that concepts of "right" and "wrong" can't be taught in public school systems. Naturally, that makes parents who believe in a certain code of ethics very nervous. The issue is control. Parents who care about their children want to be in charge when it comes to setting goals for the future, and have no intention of bowing out quietly and turning the process over to a committee.

The most helpful educational goals are usually those that zero in on specific individuals. When you look at your own children and picture each of them at age eighteen, what do you hope to see? Over the years, my own goals for the children have gradually become better defined and can now be grouped into six areas: values, attitudes, habits, skills, individual talents and interests, and general knowledge.

My Personal Goals for My Children

In the area of *values*, I hope to teach my children to care deeply about other people and the environment they live in; to develop a personal relationship with Jesus; and to live in accordance with Biblical principles.

One of the most important ***attitudes*** I hope to foster in my children is a continued love of learning. Sometimes the biggest challenge has been to avoid doing things that might damage their built-in motivation and replace it with something less worthwhile, like a love for grades, prizes, or "happy-face stickers." In this area my goals have helped me recognize what ***not*** to do. Sometimes, this can be just as important as determining what should be done.

The list of ***habits*** I've tried to develop in the children is long. Besides the obvious ones, such as punctuality, orderliness, cleanliness, and politeness, many others aren't as obvious, and can sometimes seem downright contradictory. For example, it can be difficult to balance the need for "order" with a desire to foster creativity. Certain academic habits, such as using a dictionary to find out the meaning of an unknown word or picking up an encyclopedia to learn something when it is needed, are also important and are best learned through example and modeling.

Many ***skills*** are necessary for living in today's complex world. For starters, there are "academic skills," like reading, writing, and arithmetic. To these, I would add "living skills" like interpreting an airplane schedule or making a bed; "practical skills" like woodworking or baking, and specific "vocational" or "recreational" skills like wiring a light fixture or playing a guitar. Every member of the family doesn't necessarily have to become proficient in all these skills, but I do hope to raise well-rounded children who have many abilities and the self-worth to believe that they can do anything if they try hard enough!

The category of *individual talents and interests* is most frequently overlooked by the conventional school teacher. In the home school setting, there is much more time to devote to discovering and developing individual talents. For example, our oldest son is an accomplished musician, whereas our daughter loves to work in the theatre. Our middle boy is a born athlete, and his little sister is a gifted artist. The youngest is too little to let us know yet what his particular talent will be, but I am eagerly waiting to see what direction he goes. (I think he may be leaning towards a career in demolition.)

You'll notice that I did include *knowledge* in my list of goals, but I purposely assigned it last place. For most people who are involved with traditional education, this has always been the primary goal. Personally, I've had too much experience with students who learn material, pass tests, and promptly forget everything to place my main focus on temporarily filling brain cells with irrelevant data. However, I do believe that children need to gradually build and expand their understanding of the world around them, and must be allowed to accomplish this in a way that will help them to remember the information they are gathering.

Most of the general knowledge the children learn in our home comes about through their involvement in the world, and through our frequent discussions on just about every subject under the sun. We also do a lot of reading together. They learn a great deal by watching high-quality videos, selecting their own books at the library, and studying subjects of personal interest to them. I feel confident that the knowledge base that they are gaining in this manner will never be lost, but will gradually increase and expand over time.

Methods and Materials

The methods you use for planning, instructing, and evaluating should be a natural outgrowth of your beliefs about learning and the goals you have outlined for your family. Some of you will continue to use traditional techniques like lecturing, testing, and assigning grades. Others will give the children more freedom to assume responsibility for their learning experiences. Some of you might continue to use standard texts and workbooks, and others will do unit studies, or get most of your materials from the public library. Whatever you choose, I hope you remember that curriculum development is always a ***process***, not something you do once a year at a curriculum fair!

In Conclusion

This chapter has provided a tiny introduction to the subject of educational philosophy. I hope it has whetted your desire to learn more about the subject and work on developing your own ideas about education. This is a long-term project, and your plans are likely to grow and change over the years. I'll promise you this: if you put a little thought into the subject before the next curriculum fair season, you will wind up wasting less money, and you will have a better idea what you're going to do with the materials you have purchased when you get home!

Chapter III
Setting the Stage

The stage manager occupies one of the most important positions in the theatre. She manages the day-to-day life on the set, assisting the producer with the organizational details. She supervises the construction of the set, as well as the costuming and make-up, and sets up and enforces a rehearsal schedule. She watches out for the needs of any children who are involved in the production, and makes sure they come on time and get home safely every day.

Before a play can actually begin, the set must be organized and ready. Before a home-schooling program can get going, certain organizational matters must be attended to. Since most mothers can't afford to hire separate "stage managers," these preparations remain our own responsibility. We must be sure our "set" is in readiness intellectually, emotionally, temporally, and physically before our program gets underway.

We dealt with "intellectual preparation" in the last chapter when we discussed the importance of clarifying our educational philosophies and setting a few basic goals. In this chapter, we will consider the other three areas, beginning with the importance of establishing and maintaining our own emotional balance.

Emotional Preparation

As the mother, you are the emotional heart of your family! Whenever you are upset and irritable, everyone else is affected. That's why it is extremely important that you make sure your own needs are attended to *first*. Most of you probably have a tendency to assign last priority to yourselves. Unless you have the strength and stamina to be true saints and martyrs for the cause, this can be a dreadful mistake.

To begin with, your own physical needs must be attended to. This requires a certain amount of sleep, a decent diet, and sufficient exercise to keep you "energized." Second, your need for occasional peace and quiet must somehow be satisfied. Third, you must avoid the tendency to put all of your own interests and hobbies on a shelf, thinking you no longer have any time for them.

All of this might sound selfish and impossible to achieve, especially if you have a large and lively household, with a baby and a couple of "rug-rats" toddling around in addition to your school-age youngsters. However, there is always a way to improve the situation if you assign it a high-enough priority. Occasional babysitters can be employed, older children can watch younger children, or husbands can be asked to take a turn with the little ones. Making the decision to take control over your children's education does not necessarily require that you become a total martyr to your family. If you fail to pay attention to your own needs, you will probably wind up burning out.

Besides, if you set aside every one of your own interests and hobbies, your children will grow up never really knowing who you are! Worse, they will miss many enriching learning opportunities. Remember when we were talking about motivation? One of the surest ways to share learning experiences with your children is to show them what you are excited about.

Before we had children, my husband and I were both aspiring musicians, playing in separate bands. For several years, both of us did put our interests on the shelf, while we had our first couple of babies. During that period, before any of the children were old enough to help out, it was extremely difficult to maintain a hobby that required a reasonable amount of practice. Occasionally, when the oldest became a toddler, we tried to get him interested in fooling around with an instrument, without much success. But when we began to play ourselves again, our son gradually found his own life's work! Now he lives, eats, and breathes music. He plays guitar, teaches younger children, and even makes and repairs instruments. I don't believe he would have discovered this all-consuming interest without "catching" it from our own enthusiastic participation in music.

So, if you love to read, or crochet, or do needlepoint, or raise horses, or write books, by all means, continue to participate in these things! Try to share them with your youngsters as much as possible, but don't feel guilty if you need a few minutes alone once in awhile. You may have to figure out how to accomplish things in short spurts of time, or work your own activities around your children's schedule. It can require some frustrating adjustments, but it's a lot more frustrating to give up everything! Mothers who are planning to put their children in school when they are five might be able to put their interests on a shelf and look forward to "stage two," when their kids will be out of the house. As a home-schooling mother, my "stage two" will come when I'm fifty-eight years old! I don't know about you, but I don't want to wait that long to remember what I like to do in my "spare time!"

Of course, once you have begun paying attention to your own needs, eating healthy foods, sleeping and exercising properly, and taking some time to maintain your own interests, you may no longer have any good excuses for those occasional temper tantrums! (That's right, I'm talking about you, not the two-year-old!) If you're still having some trouble in that area, it may help to try a couple of techniques I've worked out (but not necessarily perfected) over the years.

One of the most important things that I do to maintain my own emotional balance is to establish a harmonious center inside myself. For me, that center comes from taking some quiet time each day to read the Bible or pray, and seeking to find "the peace of God that passes all understanding." If you happen to feel off-balance and empty right now, I invite you to try plugging into my energy source! He has never failed to "fill me up" when I need it most!

Next, I make it a point to try to "act," rather than "react" to what is going on around me. If the toddler is screaming or my teenagers are grouchy, I keep repeating to myself, "Act, don't react." I deal with the situation, concentrating on whatever it is *I* should be doing. Eventually, everybody else gets back on track. In the past, I found myself "reacting" to such situations and getting testy. Soon the others would be going about their own business, happy as a lark, and I'd still be standing over a tub of dishes, steaming and reliving all the gory details. Finally, I just decided it wasn't worth it!

My final technique for maintaining my own balance is a simple "filing card system." Every morning, the first thing I do is to go downstairs, look over my calendar, and write down all our "external" appointments for the day on a small filing card. Then I jot down the following categories: professional; personal; housework; schoolwork; children's activities. Under each I write down whatever items will receive a high priority that day. (Sometimes a particular category will remain blank.) On the back of the card, I list these in the approximate order that I intend to do them, and then use this card as a "game plan" for the rest of the day.

I don't treat this list as an inflexible plan of action. Many days I wind up changing activities or scrapping the whole thing. However, making it helps me to notice when things are getting off balance. If I can easily come up with twenty items that must get done professionally, and can't imagine what activities the children might be doing that day, I know I've allowed my own work to become too important. If the housework is starting to go down the drain, it quickly becomes apparent. If I go for days at a time with nothing to put in the "personal" or "professional" categories, I know I've allowed my own interests to get sabotaged and am heading for "burn-out city."

These issues of maintaining balance and avoiding burn-out lead us to the next area of preparation, which is dealing with time-related, or "temporal" concerns. Children have as much need for balance as adults do, and the entire family must maintain a reasonable schedule if the production is going to be a success.

Temporal Preparation

Several years ago, in order to supplement our family income, I began teaching piano lessons in the afternoons to school children. The first thing I noticed was the "stress" factor that these children carried with them as a result of over-programming. Some of these children began the morning in day care, went to school all day long (with no recess!), and came to my piano lessons worn out, with two hours of homework left to look forward to. They had other lessons, too. Some of them took art on Mondays, piano on Tuesdays, gymnastics on Wednesdays, dance on Thursdays, and scouts on Fridays. No wonder they never had any time to practice!

One of the reasons we began home schooling was my desire for a more balanced childhood for our children. There are four areas that I believe require constant attention: academics, work, free play, and creative pursuits. In most schools, academics takes the upper hand and the rest of these needs are shortchanged. We have found that our academics can be completed in a very short period, leaving much more time for other forms of work and play.

When people have large families, like ours, it is still easy to let the schedule get out of control, however. Even one activity per child, per week, can be enough to keep the entire family from eating supper together! Because of this, it is important to continually re-think this issue of balance. Sometimes adjustments have to be made more than once a semester. In our family, we have found that iron-clad rules, like "one activity per child" just don't work. Instead, we consider individual needs, and balance the importance of personal activities with the quest for overall harmony. In baseball season, for example, our whole family gets caught up in our middle child's "fetish." We allow him to participate, even though it wreaks havoc with our schedule, because it is his number one interest. On the other hand, when our daughter decided she "would like to give softball a try," we had to say, "no." Her mild interest in the sport was not worth the increased hassle. Her primary interest is drama, however, and the whole family has sometimes gone without sufficient sleep for a week or two while she was in the middle of "production week."

On a daily basis, time management is also extremely important. We have a basic schedule but are always flexible and willing to change it around when necessary. Some people wonder what the point is in having a schedule if we are so quick to scrap it. We have found that the presence of a basic framework assures us that everything will be accomplished eventually. When we do need to make changes, at least we recognize what we are "missing," and are more apt to make it up sooner or later.

Our daily schedule during the week looks something like this:

8 a.m.	breakfast, Bible story
8:30 until 9:30 or 10	chore time
9:30 or 10 until noon	academic time
Noon until 1	lunch, free time
1 until 2	"quiet time"
2 until 5	time for errands, library trips, practices, private lessons, etc.
Evening	family or individual activities

These blocks of time are by no means inviolate. For example, if I need help with a chore in the middle of quiet time, I never hesitate to ask. If studying doesn't get done during academic time, it might be done in the evening, or during quiet time. If a tennis lesson has been re-scheduled during morning hours, academic time might come later that day. However, the basic schedule helps the children have some idea what to expect, and they know that if it gets sabotaged they will eventually have to complete their work anyway.

If you are one of the many home schoolers who have more specific schedules, with certain hours set aside for math, science, and social studies, that approach might be working well for your family. However, I have seen several home schoolers become so "locked into" their self-imposed schedules that they won't take advantage of spontaneous learning experiences or use their freedom to enjoy life outdoors on a beautiful spring day. To me, that suggests they have little control over their own educational programs. I hope you will avoid following in their footsteps. After all, what is the point of being a home schooler if you can't enjoy the "fruits" of the flexibility you have managed to obtain?

Physical Organization

Many authors have discussed household management and organization, so I'm going to keep this section brief. When it comes to housekeeping, my main concern is underlying cleanliness and basic order. It doesn't bother me if our house occasionally looks like a tornado hit it, as long as 1) I know that, deep down, the bathroom and kitchen are reasonably clean; and 2) people will know where things belong when it is time to straighten up again.

The issue of housework is one where many people go to extremes. I have been in houses where the mothers have given up and turned their kitchen over to the roaches. On the other hand, there are some homes where so much attention is paid to housework that little else can be accomplished, and "creative urges" are never given free rein. Things are given a higher priority than people.

In our home, the children are expected to kick in and do their fair share of the housework. That means that I must be willing to spend a little time training someone to do a job, and must then relax my standards in order to resist the urge to do it over again.

When it comes to "work," individual differences can be seen at their finest. One of our boys was born with a mop in his hand. His room is always clean, his books are alphabetized, and his collections are catalogued. When given an assignment, he is through within seconds and ready for more. Another one of our children can spend thirty minutes taking the garbage to the street. (Of course, he may have figured out a new mathematical proof or written a song on the way.) In the short run, dealing with reluctant participants can drive you crazy, but in the long-run, the continuous attempt to instruct, delegate, and teach responsibility will pay off. (At least, I keep telling myself that!)

Psychologically, it has always helped me to have one time of day when I strive for complete order. Sometimes, that has been in the morning right after chore time, or the late afternoon, just before my husband returns from the office. When the children were younger, it was in the evening just after we put them to bed. Rather than picking up all day long, and re-doing the same chores fifteen times, getting total order just once a day helps me remember that there really is hope.

As for "underlying cleanliness," I try to do one major cleaning chore a week. Now that the children are older, they sometimes take a turn doing this chore. One week it might be scrubbing the bathroom thoroughly, and another week it might be cleaning out the kitchen cabinets. I'm sure my mother would pass out if she thought this meant my bathroom is only cleaned once every two months, but I'm talking about deep down cleaning, not just a little "surface wiping and swiping." If each of the important areas in my home is cleaned deep down once every month or two, I consider that "spotless" enough.

In order to establish basic order so that we know where everything belongs, I have needed to overcome my own tendency to become a "pack rat," by periodically going around and throwing away items or giving them to Goodwill. Although the children have gradually improved in their own ability to organize their rooms, they can easily become overwhelmed if they have too many clothes or toys. After I have gone through their rooms with them, getting rid of a lot of things and helping them to arrange the rest in an orderly manner, they have a much easier time keeping things straight themselves.

After you have the house organized and have some kind of a scheme for keeping it reasonably clean, it's time to consider your "academic environment." Some parents actually try to set up a "school room," complete with individual desks, blackboards on the walls, and a globe on the teacher's work table. That approach has never worked for us. Our academic materials are spread out all over the house.

I'd like to make two suggestions. The first is simple, but it took me a long time to learn. If things are down low and accessible, and children have permission to take them out without asking, the materials will get used. If they are stored up high, to be used when the "teacher" plans an activity, they will be used much less. It has taken me awhile to get comfortable with seeing expensive encyclopedias lying open on the floor with a toddler dancing on top of them. However, I'd rather have them be used, (or even abused), than to see them sitting on the shelf.

My second suggestion concerns the arrangement of your home into "learning centers." Learning centers are basically small areas that are set up with a particular subject area (or a specific topic) in mind. For example, we have an "art center," where all the art materials are kept. There is a place on the wall for exhibiting the latest creations, and a section for art books and a few classical reproductions. Our "language arts" center is near the computer, where the dictionaries, thesauruses, extra paper and pencils, and other writing materials are stored. Other people have set up centers that are based on "units," or specific individual interests, such as "dinosaurs," or "nature collections."

If you'd like more information on the subject, I've written a booklet entitled, "How to Set Up Learning Centers in Your Home." It explains the concept thoroughly, lists ideas and materials for a wide variety of specific centers, and is available from the address at the back of the book.

In Conclusion

Now that you are thoroughly prepared, it is time for the curtain to rise on "act one" of your production. If your children are still young, the first item on your agenda will probably be teaching them to read and write. Some of you may wonder how you will manage to accomplish something that seems to give trained educators so much trouble. Yet you may also question, "Can it really be that difficult to teach a subject that some children have learned all by themselves?" In the next chapter, let's start by exploding a few myths!

Chapter IV
Act I: Natural Literacy

My son Steve just had his third birthday two days ago, and he is still talking baby-talk. If a "language expert" came to our house, the child would almost certainly be labeled "language-delayed." As a mother, I recognize that he is a little slow compared to the others, but I'm also confident that, within a year, I will be wishing he would be quiet from time to time!

For a moment, imagine the following scenario. Suppose a group of experts got together and decided a particular set of skills was required in order for children to demonstrate "talking readiness." To begin with, parents would be encouraged to have their children watch educational television programs (and, of course, buy the corresponding workbooks) in order to teach their children the "beginning sounds." Then, after the children had demonstrated they were "ready to learn to talk," they would be allowed to enroll in "talking school" at precisely the age of 2.3. There, talking would be introduced using the "modern skills approach," where all speech would be broken down into its smallest components and presented in a completely disconnected manner. Grades and prizes would be given to the best talkers so that the children would soon forget that they had any other reason for learning to speak besides competing for the teacher's recognition. Instruction would be given to all students, including those who were already speaking, in order to make sure that no one had missed any essential "skills." Of course, some students would be bored. However, the parents would be promised that individualized attention would be provided and that those who were already talking would focus on "talking comprehension," so they could make sense of the language they were already using. Furthermore, parents would be assured that testing would commence shortly, and any "gifted talkers" would be given two hours of special instruction once a week, where they would be encouraged to use their talking skills in a creative group situation. Some children, of course, might not be ready for the skills instruction yet, so they would be labeled "talking disabled" and assigned to special classes or taken out of the room once a week for remedial attention. Within a few years, lawmakers would bow to pressure from the "language lobby," and begin to require attendance at talking school for all 2.3 year olds. At this point, a few concerned parents would begin signing up for home talking programs. However, their curricula would be carefully monitored by teams of "talking specialists" who would claim the right to visit the parents in their homes to oversee the operation.

Does all of this sound a trifle absurd? It's no more ridiculous than the corresponding emphasis on "teaching children to read" that currently exists in the public school system! In a literate home, in a literate society, learning to read and write should be every bit as "normal" a process as learning to talk or to walk! There is absolutely no need to purchase expensive curricula or set aside special times for "skills instruction."

This assertion is not based on some theoretical, pie-in-the-sky formula. It stems from personal experience in the field. My four older children are all reading and writing far above their "grade levels," and they have never been "taught" to read in the manner of other school children. More important, they all *love* to read and do it constantly. They do it for enjoyment and to learn information they need, and they do it without assignments or bribery of any kind! Most of the books they choose are high-quality children's literature or "classics" by authors like Charles Dickens or Samuel Clemens. They developed these high standards by having good books read to them when they were younger, and by gradually being allowed to select their own reading materials.

Of course, from time to time, they also slip in a few "junk books." After all, they are human! Once in awhile, I do need to step in and suggest that they might be getting stuck in a rut. At that point, I sometimes ask them to "take turns," or read a certain number of classics each semester, along with their other books. Generally, they get back on track with little coercion. For the most part, they have all demonstrated excellent taste, and take out a variety of materials from the library without being forced.

All of this was accomplished without the use of workbooks, book reports, or instruction in "reading comprehension." We never used a store-bought phonics curriculum, or read basal readers, except for fun. Of course, we did sometimes *buy* workbooks and phonics curricula in the early years, but they always wound up sitting on the shelf! I guess we were just too busy going to the library and *reading* to use them!

The "War on Illiteracy"

Why do educators make such a big deal about "teaching reading," if it can actually be learned this effortlessly? Why is there so much adult illiteracy in today's world? Why do teachers seem to have so much trouble in schools with "slow readers"? Why is the number of children labeled "learning disabled" growing larger every year? There are four reasons I can think of for all this fuss and bother.

Illiterate Homes

First of all, reading only comes naturally in families that value literacy. Unfortunately, many children grow up in homes that are disadvantaged. They have no adult role models who are reading books or taking them to the library. There are few magazines and books available for them to use. Television broadcasts have taken the place of newspapers, and evenings are spent in front of the "boob tube."

Back in the sixties and seventies, educators decided that something should be done to give such disadvantaged children a "head start" on education. Early preschool programs were funded during the "War on Poverty," and programs like Sesame Street were started to help such children learn their numbers, alphabet, and beginning reading skills. Thirty years later, the reviews are mixed concerning the long-range effects of these programs on such disadvantaged children. Some research indicates these programs have had a dramatic effect. Other research points back to the need for intervening in the home lives of the children in order for any true progress to be made.

Whatever results these programs have demonstrated for the disadvantaged children in our society, they have dramatically changed life for *all* children. With the advent of preschools and programs like Sesame Street, most parents have gradually accepted the "fact" that their children need this kind of instruction during the preschool years in order to "compete" later. The workbooks and tapes that were originally designed for children who had no literate role models at home have gradually crept into the homes of children who had perfectly great role models to begin with!

The idea that three-year-olds need instruction to recognize the "front" and the "back" of a book, or that parents must "teach" their children to cut with a scissors or color within the lines are examples of the notions that have been popularized by many day care operators. In a literate home, teaching such "readiness skills" is totally unnecessary. If you provide the necessary tools and equipment and are available to answer questions and provide help when they ask for it, your children will acquire these "readiness" skills with minimal assistance when the time is right for *them*.

Motivational Techniques that Backfire

The second reason for all the illiteracy in America stems from the way "motivation" is handled in the schools. Most of you are familiar with two-year-olds, who want to learn *everything!* Just one two-year-old child has enough internal motivation for a whole classroom of fifth graders. Why do so many ten-year-olds in conventional schools lack motivation? What happens in between that changes them? After all, there's no rule that says ten-year-olds aren't supposed to enjoy reading! My ten-year-old loves to read. Why do so many of his friends who go to school view it as an unpleasant assignment?

Their own motivation has been systematically destroyed! In the early grades they are seldom allowed to read what they *want* to read. Many of the stories they are given are insipid and dull, and the textbooks are "dumbed down" until they are completely mindless. Even if an occasional story is interesting, the children are required to answer questions, write reports, and dissect the action until they become so sick of books they want to scream! Then, when it is clear that they no longer view reading as an enjoyable experience, the teachers feel a need to stir up their motivation again by dangling external motivators in front of them. Gradually, the children come to concentrate on contests, grades, "happy face" (or "frowny face"!) stickers, excessive praise, and the need to avoid punishment, rather than on their own desire to read for enjoyment. By that point, "reading" is usually viewed as something that is done only under duress, in school. Television or video games become their preferred activities during leisure time. By the time these children reach the fifth grade, they have already been thoroughly programmed to dislike reading and will be likely to pass on that dislike to the next generation of non-readers.

My own children have loved to read from a very early age. By the time my oldest son was eight he was reading beginning classics, like *Tom Sawyer*. Every summer, though, when the "summer reading program" at the library began, he immediately started reading short, dumb books, in order to rack up "points" and earn prizes. Some motivation! We wound up with a bunch of "parachutes" hanging off his "airplane" from the middle of the library ceiling. Forget about meaningful reading experiences! He was too busy collecting parachutes to care about books! It didn't take too long for me to learn to avoid these "motivational" programs like the plague!

One Timetable; One Method

The third reason for the illiteracy problem is the way schools force children to learn on rigid timetables, using the same methods for all children, even if they are not appropriate for particular individuals. When children are allowed to learn at their own pace, the age they begin to read varies tremendously. My first son learned at age four, and my second son at age seven. There is no reason to believe that all children will learn at exactly 6.5 years of age, during the first grade, other than the convenience of the reading teacher.

Most of my children have learned to read by sounding out letters, using real books and a few simple phonics games that were available to them in the home. However, one of my daughters, who is now thirteen years old, might never have learned if I had insisted she use phonics. Some children cannot hear those sounds, no matter how hard they try! She learned mainly through memorization and recognizing the shapes of the words. Allowing her to use this approach resulted in a few interesting spelling mistakes during the early years, but she is a wonderful reader now. In the long run, her chosen method has not had a single negative effect. If she had been in the schools, the teachers might have forced her to fit into a different mold, thereby "creating" all kinds of learning disabilities. By this time, she might be a basket case, instead of someone who absolutely adores books! (Of course, the same thing might have happened if the phonetic learners in the family had been forced to learn through the "whole word approach.")

True Learning Disabilities

The final cause of illiteracy is the presence of a true learning disability. This is very, very rare! If all children were allowed to learn in their own way, on their own timetables, the "learning disabilities classes" would have a hard time filling their quotas. Although there are some people with genuine difficulties, I believe the "natural" approach would work for them, too. It might take them considerably longer, but the results would almost certainly be better than if they were tested, labeled, segregated into separate groups, and treated as if they had some deadly affliction!

While writing this chapter, I received a phone call from a woman who has three children. One is an average learner, one is autistic, and the third has an "attention deficit disorder." We discussed her perceived need for outside help. She mentioned an interesting "rule of thumb" for helping parents determine whether or not their children have true learning disorders. She suggested that learning disorders are probably "real" if the parents notice specific problems themselves when the children are babies or preschoolers. "Disabilities" that first become noticeable after the children are placed in school have probably been caused by the group setting and are likely to disappear if the children are brought back home.

Sometimes it may be necessary for parents to search for assistance when they cannot deal with a situation on their own. There is nothing inherently wrong with this, as long as the parents remain in control and can determine the amount and type of assistance they receive. However, whenever authorities suspect possible "learning disabilities" or "handicaps," they often try to take over and displace the parents as managers. For this reason, I urge all parents to exercise caution and look into such programs discreetly before they get anyone else involved.

Learning to Read: The Parent's Role

If you don't need to "teach your children to read" using lesson plans and expensive curriculum materials, does that mean you have no role at all to play in the process? Certainly not! You are still an important player, and your own attitude towards reading is extremely important!

Your initial focus must be on creating a literate environment in your own home. In order to do this, you need to take time to look at books and magazines yourself! When the children view the reading process as an important part of the grown-up world, they will want to join in as soon as possible.

The next important step is to read books to your children, beginning when they are toddlers. Start with interesting books with plenty of pictures. Later, as their attention spans improve, you can gradually switch to higher-quality children's literature, and then move on to adult classics. Many parents stop reading to their children as soon as they are capable of reading on their own. This is a serious mistake! When you continue to read to the children on a level that is slightly higher than their own ability allows, you help them improve their vocabularies and listening skills, and motivate them to try reading difficult books on their own.

The third important component is to provide a variety of materials that will stimulate their interest in reading. In addition to books and magazines of their own, they should have a regular library trip to look forward to. Related games and materials should also be available on a low shelf, where they will be able to use them when the spirit moves. It is not necessary to spend a lot of money to accomplish this. One of the most important tools my children used when they were learning to read was a simple hand-made phonics game that had a number of different word-parts to put together. For example, they could put "g" with "ood" to make "good;" or combine "sh with oot" to make "shoot." After awhile, they moved up to store-bought games like "Scrabble," or "Upwords." They also made good use of a preschool dictionary that was purchased for $2 at Wal-Mart. The only item that consistently remained on the shelf in "brand-new condition" was the $100 phonics curriculum I bought the first year of home schooling! I guess it looked too "educational" to catch their eye!

Of course, these phonics games were completely useless in the case of my oldest daughter. She learned in a different manner altogether. One year when she was about six, we sat on the couch together day after day, reading the same books over and over at her request. I could just "feel" the intensity with which she was focusing on the text and memorizing the words. In order to speed the process up a little, we also made a few "word cards" together, and kept them in a small file box. On these cards, we did things like draw a face on the "g" at the beginning of the word girl, and make the "H" of house into a little house, with a stairway going up to the second floor. I'm not sure these "props" were necessary. It was probably just a case of overkill on my part. As usual, when things did "click" for her, it appeared to be completely magical. One day she couldn't read, and a few days later, she could! Once she got going, there was no stopping her!

Despite the importance of providing for the needs of children with divergent learning styles, it's not really necessary to spend much time "diagnosing" or "labeling" them. As long as you provide a variety of materials and experiences, and children are free to make their own choices, they will automatically select those items that will work best for them. When parents have accepted the value of allowing children to learn on their own in this manner, they sometimes go overboard and purposefully avoid instigating learning experiences themselves. There's never any harm in offering to help a youngster read a story, or asking them if they'd like to play a particular phonics game! The harm comes from "forcing" these activities when the children aren't interested! Often when this happens, it's because the children are not yet ready for a particular experience. If you try something and it doesn't seem to be working, you can always back down and try something a little different later. That's one of the benefits of home schooling. No mother will intentionally keep doing something if it becomes clear it is hurting her children! A little judicious "quitting" does not have to be an indication of failure in the long run!

Another thing you can do for your children is provide them with a variety of background experiences. These are absolutely vital to children who are learning how to read. If a child has never been to a zoo to see an elephant, he will not be able to make sense out of a story like "Dumbo." If he has never seen the inside of a train station, he will have difficulty understanding *The Train to Timbuctoo*. If he has never been to a farm, he will have trouble visualizing the life portrayed in Laura Ingalls Wilder's "Little House" series. Family outings are usually preferable to large-scale field trips, because the pace can be more leisurely. Besides, the children tend to pay more attention to the experience, and less to the tomfoolery going on around them.

As the children become a bit more proficient at reading, it is time for them to start becoming acquainted with reference materials. Again, this is best learned from observing role models who demonstrate how to look up information when it is really needed. In our home, the children are constantly looking things up in the encyclopedia. They didn't learn this from a "unit" on reference skills. They learned it from watching their father, who, in turn, got the habit from his parents! In the same manner, they have learned to locate unknown places on a map or globe when the need arises. Sometimes I get very paranoid when I see that $50 globe being passed back and forth in the living room, but it wouldn't be worth 5 cents sitting on top of the file cabinet safe and sound.

The Reading Road to Writing

Hmm ...Does that sound backwards to you? It doesn't to me! I have found children who learn to enjoy reading will eventually develop into wonderful writers all by themselves! However, with certain kids, it might take awhile! When my oldest son, Sam, was in sixth grade, he had extreme difficulty coming up with a paragraph that made any sense at all. At the same time, he was bringing home library books like *Robinson Crusoe* and *Watership Down*, which are written on an adult level. At first I couldn't understand how he could be so great at reading, and so hopelessly inept at writing! Gradually, however, it began to dawn on me. It was precisely *because* he was so good at reading that he hated to write! He *felt* inept! He recognized he was capable of reading things like, "This is the forest primeval, the murmuring pines and the hemlocks," and was incapable of writing anything beyond the level of, "I like my dog. My dog's name is Buffy." It's no wonder he got very little satisfaction from the process!

When Sam reached the seventh grade, something suddenly "clicked." Within a few months, he had finished writing an entire novel with eighteen chapters! It had obviously taken that long to have the writing process "jell" inside his mind. Once he got started, the words just seemed to overflow onto the paper! Because he had not been subjected to endless "writing exercises" as a younger child, and had "learned" to read and write at the hands of masters like Charles Dickens and Jules Verne, he quickly developed a unique style of his own. By the time he entered tenth grade, he knew how to write both fiction and non-fiction reports better than most college students, and completed his first term paper with little difficulty.

Sam was the only one of our children who followed this rather circuitous method of learning how to write. The others have developed their skills much more gradually, following a fairly predictable pattern. After they learned to recognize the alphabet, their next step was to pass through the "drive Mom crazy" stage. This stage was characterized by conversations like the following:

"Mommy, can I write a letter to Sophia?"

"Sure, honey. I'll be glad to help."

"What should I say?"

"How about starting with "Dear Sophia...""

"Okay, how do you spell "dear"?

"D-e..."

"Wait! Wait! How do you make a d?"

One of the next stages on their road to literacy was the "copying stage." During this period, the children would take several pages and staple them together, announcing that they were "going to write a book." Then they would laboriously trace all the pictures from a library book and copy the complete story, word for word. Sometimes they would sit at the computer, and do a similar stunt using the keyboard. At that time, they usually had to hunt and peck for each key, and it often took them several weeks to copy a long book onto their personal disks. The books themselves were often too difficult for them to read, and they sometimes asked me to read the stories back to them in order to "listen to" what they were "writing!"

My daughter Laura, who is the most talented artist in the family, is now using a similar technique for learning to draw. Sometimes, for days at a time, she buries herself in her art corner and "traces" one picture after another in her notebook. Then, just as I become convinced that all creativity has permanently gone down the tubes, she emerges from her latest "copying stage" and goes back to creative drawing. Usually the experience with the tracing paper has propelled her to a higher skill level. In the same way, copying stories seems to help the children achieve a higher level of performance in writing whenever they are ready to return to creative work.

Learning to Write: The Parent's Role

You can do several things to assist your children as they are developing their writing skills. First, you can act as a role model. When I was writing and publishing my dissertation, all of the children were very involved in the process. It wasn't long afterwards that Sam went on his "writing binge" in seventh grade. My own writing appeared to be one of the forces that led to his love affair with the computer. If the children observe you writing letters to your friends, they will be more inclined to find penpals of their own. If they see you writing articles and submitting them to magazines, they will often try to do the same, especially if you happen to meet with any success!

The second thing you can do is to provide them with writing materials and be available to provide assistance when it is requested. One of the first "learning centers" that we developed at our house was a "writing center." We keep notebooks, paper, pens and pencils, envelopes and stamps all in one place, where the children can use them whenever they wish. This center is located near the computer, and we also have an electronic typewriter that seems to be preferred by the younger children.

Some people are afraid that children who are allowed to use typewriters and computers will never develop their penmanship skills.   This has never concerned me. For one thing, penmanship has never been high on my own list of goals for the children. I value the communication itself, rather than the "style," and tend to use the computer for most of my own writing. Although we have tried to encourage the children to develop legible styles of writing, we have never placed a great deal of importance on the subject. If you do decide to teach penmanship in your home, I hope you will call it "penmanship," instead of "writing." When the two are viewed as distinct subjects, there is less tendency for boredom with "writing practice" to transfer to the "real thing."

When our middle son, Dan, began to learn how to print the alphabet, I was temporarily distracted because I was in the throes of studying for the exit exams for my Ph.D. By the time I came up for air, he had taught himself how to print and had learned it "wrong." He started most of his letters at the bottom and was going completely opposite to those cute little arrows in the composition books. For weeks, I agonized over the situation. As an educator, I felt like grabbing the pencil and showing him how to do it "right." As a mother, I knew that he would back into a corner and regress if I tried to mess with him. It took a long time for me to recognize that he was having no difficulty at all with his unique system. In fact, he was rapidly developing the best handwriting in the whole family. So what if he was doing it "wrong"? It worked for him! Right now, in the middle of the fifth grade, he is occupied with teaching himself cursive. This time he is doing it "right," using a book and following the arrows precisely. He is doing this completely on his own initiative, and seems to feel a greater need to "conform" this time around.

As my children have grown, my own role has gradually evolved into that of an "editor." As in the real world, however, I wait until my authors request assistance with their work. Then I usually sit at the computer with them, pointing out misspellings or grammatical errors, and making a few suggestions like, "This doesn't seem clear to me, here. What were you trying to get at?"

When you reach this point, two things might be helpful. First, if you haven't already developed your own skills as a writer and editor, you need to work on them! Second, it might help to have the children go through a "crash course," like "Winston Grammar" when they are in about sixth or seventh grade. This will introduce them to words like "nouns," "verbs," "antecedents," etc.," which are helpful to understand when working with an editor.

In Conclusion

Reading and writing are probably the most important subjects in the primary grades. However, they are just the first steps in obtaining a well-rounded education. In the next chapter, we will turn our attention to the development of a "living curriculum." Let's forget about having an intermission and go right on to "Act Two"!

Chapter V
Act II: A Living Curriculum

Most home schoolers associate the word "curriculum" with the spring curriculum fairs that have become popular throughout the country. They think of a "curriculum" as a set of materials that they purchase for a particular year. One of them asks, "What curriculum will you be using?," and the other answers, "Bob Jones," "Abeka," or "We're doing unit studies this year."

Actually, "curriculum development" does not refer to the selection of a set of materials. It is a *process* that begins with the consideration of your educational philosophy. Remember back in chapter two, when we discussed the importance of defining goals, considering your ideas about learning, analyzing the teacher/student relationship, and deciding upon methods of planning, instruction, and evaluation? These are the underlying steps in curriculum development. After all these steps have been taken, then and only then is anyone really prepared to plan or select a curriculum.

Most people also think of a curriculum as something that has to be divided into mutually discrete "subject areas." They ask questions like, "What are you doing in science this year?" or "Which math curriculum are you using?" This approach, while popular, is only one possible way to view the process of curriculum development.

Our family believes in using a *living* curriculum that does not break up the real world into bits and pieces known as "subject areas." We do not set up a compartmentalized time schedule, where "science" is studied from 10:00 to 11:00, and social studies from 11:00 to 12:00. We use few texts, except in the upper levels of math. We don't set out to design specific units of study, either. We allow the curriculum to "flow" out of everyday life. It generally revolves around current events taking place in the world, (or sometimes on the television screen or in a book), and around the current interests of the members of the family, including the adults.

Although we don't focus on specific "subject areas" when learning experiences are taking place, we have to be able to answer the inevitable questions like, "What did you do in science and social studies this year?" when the school board supervisor comes at the end of the year. In the final chapter, I'll explain how we manage to keep records and prepare for these periodic "reviews." For now, I'm going to try to break down our curriculum into individual subject areas in order to explain what we do. It's important to remember, however, that we think of this curriculum as "integrated," and don't try to put up artificial walls to partition one section of life from another.

Science

Most home-schooling parents can be broken down into two groups when it comes to their approach to science: those who use textbooks and those who believe in "hands-on learning." Most of the latter group depend heavily on the use of experiments and buy a variety of booklets and materials that stress the importance of "active learning."

The trouble with using science texts is that most of them are extremely boring. They are written using "scientific jargon" which can be difficult for children to understand. Students using such texts often learn just enough to repeat the material on a test, and then promptly forget everything.

Did you ever study a chemistry textbook during high school? I did. Do you remember anything about it? I don't. I remember there was a big chart on the wall and my partner and I once almost blew up the lab, but that's about it. Would you be able to stand up and give a fifteen-minute lecture on the basics of chemistry? If you can honestly answer "yes," I'm willing to bet that you're either a chemistry freak or you just studied the subject again with your child!

At first glance, the "hands-on," experimental approach seems to be much more productive. The students usually enjoy doing the experiments and seem to be increasing their understanding of the natural world. They also tend to remember more when they have actually participated in an experiment. However, there can be pitfalls when using this method, too.

Parents who use the experimental approach often teach in a very disconnected fashion. They jump from magnetism to "building a volcano" to "backyard science" to "kitchen science" and back again. Children need to construct their own understanding of the world one link at a time. They are constantly building on previous information when they are attempting to make sense of current input. Presenting them with a series of pre-planned, unrelated experiments may not be the best way to accomplish this.

The experiment books also have one very common "flaw." Most of them include the answers, and usually give them on the same page as the experiment itself! A true scientist is supposed to observe, to consider, to think up hypotheses, and to prove or disprove his own theories. He isn't supposed to look at the bottom of the page to find out what just happened! If you do use this method, it would be wise to copy your experiments onto separate cards, and keep a firm grasp on your lips to avoid "telling" anyone what is going on too soon. Give them some time to try to figure things out on their own, even if their "hypotheses" seem a little weird. After all, Galileo and Einstein didn't start out with all the right answers, either.

Learning the "scientific method" (observing, hypothesizing, experimenting, etc.) is a very important part of the science curriculum. However, this must be taught incidentally, during the actual process of doing science. Actually, small children use the scientific method naturally, even if they can't explain what they are doing. If you observe a two-year-old in the bathtub, you can clearly see this method at work.

Our oldest son once went to school for three months to "see what it was like." Before he left home, science was one of his favorite subjects. When he returned, he announced that science was his "worst subject" and he "hated it." After we questioned him, we learned the teacher had spent three months "teaching" the scientific method without allowing the students to do any experiments! Every time he heard the word "hypothesis," his face turned green. It was about two years before he could once again participate in science activities at home and enjoy them.

When I consider our "science curriculum," I try to focus on the real purposes for studying this subject. The first is to increase awareness of the physical environment. Young children are naturally curious. Given opportunities to explore, they will gradually build their knowledge of the outdoors and learn to enjoy science. For that reason, we spend a lot of time in the woods and the fields. We go outside on a starry night and look at the constellations or listen to the crickets. We garden together, talking about the role of the worms and the "good" and "bad" insects. We study the effects of sunlight, rain, and fertilizers on the growth of the plants. We make collections and capture fireflies or butterflies. We make birdfeeders and try to identify the birds who come to eat there, varying the types of seeds and keeping charts to see who eats what. My husband takes the children fishing and dissects the catch afterwards to see what the fish were eating. We go to a variety of habitats like shores, marshes, deserts, or forests, and observe the differences in animal and plant life. When we can't visit certain areas in person, we go to places like botanical gardens, aquariums, or science museums, and view these habitats in artificial settings.

We also consider science in everyday situations, like in the bathtub or the kitchen. For the most part, the children themselves supply the questions to ponder, especially when they are little. Why does the cake rise when it is in the oven? Why does the soap float? Why does a big bubble come up when we shove a glass upside down to the bottom of the tub and then tip it on its side?

The second point of science is to help children learn to think like scientists. We are careful to avoid giving answers too quickly. Sometimes the children make up their own hypotheses. After awhile, they might realize themselves why their ideas couldn't be correct. Then they make new hypotheses, and think some more. At some point, we occasionally do go to books to find answers, or just tell them the "right answer" if we happen to know it, but we never do it right away. Children need time to think about their questions on their own.

Rather than using textbooks in science, we go to the library and take out a variety of books on scientific subjects. Sometimes the children choose these books on their own, and sometimes I'll grab a handful in the hope that they will pick them up and enjoy them. We subscribe to a variety of science magazines, like **Ranger Rick**, **National Geographic World**, **Your Big Backyard**, **Nature Friend**, and **3-2-1 Contact**. We also have a complete set of "field guides" at home, so we can identify the birds, flowers, rocks, and insects that we encounter.

Our activities are usually project-oriented, and stem from somebody's current interest. When spring comes, and I smell the earth being turned, I've got to go out into the garden, and I usually take at least one child along. When my husband gets the urge to take out the old fishing pole, he trots down to the pond with a few kids in tow, to discuss spawning and weed identification. When one of the children gets into birdwatching, we bring out the binoculars and the guide book, and go purchase a new bag of seed. When one of the children gets a brainstorm, we start a new project, like creating a "nature trail" in the woods behind our home and making a guide book to identify the things we find there. As a result of participating in these kinds of activities, we are all developing a solid understanding of science. Although we don't intend to turn them into science scholars, the children are also gradually building a core of knowledge that has enabled them to score well on the science portion of the few standardized tests they have participated in.

Math

For the most part, our family has used a typical "textbook approach" in math, especially in the upper grades. For some unfathomable reason, my younger children enjoy using math workbooks. If they didn't, I wouldn't really see the need for them in the primary grades. From fifth grade on, however, I don't know of any reasonable alternative to the use of textbooks for math. Our choice for the upper grades has been the "Saxon" series. We like its sequential approach, which builds in plenty of review, and I also enjoy having the answers in the back, so the kids can check their own work. We don't use any tests (other than a *very* occasional standardized test at the end of the year) and the older children don't even need to show me their work more than once or twice a year. They come to me occasionally to ask questions, or to request permission to "skip a section" that they already know, but other than that they are pretty much on their own. I trust them to do their work. Besides, they understand that they need to learn math in order to pass certain tests that are necessary to meet their personal goals in life. For these reasons, we have never experienced any problems with "cheating." I don't feel the need to have them take tests, either, because they obviously understand the work they are doing.

In the primary grades, math workbooks are really quite unnecessary. The concepts that need to be learned before fourth or fifth grade are very easily learned through everyday living. One of the first concepts that must be learned is the idea of 1:1 correspondence. This is crucial so that children begin to learn what numbers really represent. If they can "say" their numbers in a sing-song manner it doesn't necessarily mean they understand what those numbers actually stand for.

One-to-one correspondence can be taught in a variety of ways. One of the easiest ways is to have the children help set the table. You can ask, "How many people will be at the table tonight? Five? Okay, please get the knives and forks you will need." By doing this, the children will gradually figure out that five people need five plates, five glasses, and five sets of silverware.

As soon as children have grasped the idea that numbers stand for real quantities, they need to have a variety of concrete experiences using those numbers. They can work with fractions in the kitchen and learn important concepts while "doubling" or "halving" recipes. Learning about real money can be accomplished by giving them a small allowance, especially if they are asked to keep track of where their money goes. Telling time can best be learned gradually, by simply answering their questions, and asking them to tell you the time occasionally, assuming you're not in any particular hurry to find out the correct answer. Measurement can be learned through experiences with sewing, woodworking, map-making, or gardening.

With simple operations, like adding, subtracting, multiplying, and dividing, many math games accomplish the same purpose as traditional, boring drills. Math bingo or lotto games can either be purchased or created. Our boys loved a commercial game called, "math baseball." Flash cards or "learning wrap-ups" can be used as supplements. We also had a wonderful tape which taught the multiplication tables using sing-a-longs.

Many home schoolers today use a variety of "manipulatives" to teach primary math. Such manipulatives can be useful because young children need concrete experiences before they can begin to do operations in their head. However, these store-bought manipulatives can cost a lot of money, and they aren't really necessary. Children learned to count on their fingers long before someone thought up the need for "manipulatives." (There's really no reason to discourage "finger math," either. They will outgrow it in their own sweet time.) Simple popsicle sticks can also be used to teach such concepts as "borrowing" or "carrying." They can be bundled in groups of ten. Then, if the children need to "borrow" a group of ten, they can take one bundle apart and put the ten individual pieces in the "ones column." We used to get a big sheet of paper and divide it up into three columns, for the hundreds, tens, and ones, and do problems using Cheerios or raisins. Afterwards the children would have fun "eating" their math problems. You can't do that with plastic tubes!

If you do want to use textbooks (or discount store workbooks, which are lot cheaper), there are a couple of things that should be considered. First of all, children obviously respond to simple, colorful illustrations. They also work better when the pages are not too cluttered with problems, and when the problems that are grouped together are fairly similar. Be sure that plenty of review is built in. If it is not, add the review yourself. Whenever we learned the multiplication tables using a textbook, we actually started weeks before the textbook authors were planning to start and kept on working on these tables for several weeks afterwards.

You also need to be aware that young children, especially first and second graders, still "think" a little differently than adults. They have a very difficult time turning concepts around in their heads or considering several concepts at a time. For this reason, they may have no trouble with a problem that reads, "2+5=___," but not be able to do one that says "2+___=7." They see the "2" and the "7," and tend to put them together with the plus sign to come up with "9."

Many of the early workbooks also include "number lines," which contain operations that some children cannot comprehend. We always just skipped over those number line problems during the early years. They can "catch up" later, in about fourth grade, when they are ready for that kind of thinking. In measurement problems, many children also have difficulty because they don't really understand the underlying concepts. If two ropes are pictured, and they look about the same size, except that one is curled up tighter than the other, few children in first or second grade will understand that one is really longer. If several rulers are pictured on a page, and they are not all lined up so that their beginning edges are together, most children will not notice. They will simply look at the far edge of the rulers, and make their assumptions based on incomplete information. They tend to understand better when using real rulers and measuring real objects, but some might still have trouble.

Even after children have passed the early grades, it is important to continue to supplement the textbook approach with "real-life math." Sometime during high school, I always use a consumer math text and have the kids do some work for our business. They sit at booths at curriculum fairs, taking in money and keeping the books. They must also keep their own accounts in order, showing what they earn and where their money has gone. They are taught to tithe 10% of their earnings, and use some of the rest to establish a savings program. We also involve the older ones when we are doing our income taxes, help them learn how to do comparison shopping, and work with them at establishing their own checking accounts as soon as they are ready.

Social Studies

"Social studies" is a broad subject area which includes such topics as history, physical and cultural geography, economics, political science, sociology, and anthropology. In many elementary schools, teachers focus on the study of "communities" in the early years. They stress active learning, taking the children to fire stations, police stations, and farmer's markets. Afterwards, they come back to the classroom to participate in "dramatic play," where they dress up and pretend to be community workers.

While there is nothing inherently wrong with that approach, many schools have focused so much on experiential learning that they have neglected solid teaching in the areas of history and geography. For many years, most American school children have been virtually illiterate in these subjects. Many do not even know that Mexico is just south of the United States. I remember being appalled when a group of third-grade girl scouts had trouble distinguishing between civil and revolutionary war heroes during a discussion several years ago. More recently, with the advent of television shows and computer games like, "Where in the World is Carmen Sandiego?," educators have been attempting to correct such deficiencies. (However, if the proponents of outcomes-based education have their way, we may soon find the presentation of a solid base of knowledge on such topics taking a back seat to other objectives once again!)

As in most other subjects, we don't use textbooks to teach history or geography because they are usually boring and cover subjects in a very shallow manner. We prefer to use what some people call "living books." These include biographies of people who lived in a variety of time periods and in various places, historical fiction books, journals and diaries, and a variety of "commentaries."

This year, for example, our high schoolers are studying two books. The first is Peter Marshall's book, *The Light and the Glory*, which discusses American history from a distinctly Christian perspective. The second is Howard Zinn's, *A People's History of the United States*, which takes the viewpoint of the American Indians and other groups of people who were on the "receiving end" of the colonization experience. In studying two such disparate books, I'm hoping the children will begin to understand the necessity of knowing an author's point of view before believing everything they read. I don't want them to think everything that is labeled "historical" must necessarily be accurate.

We also watch quite a few videos or television shows that are historical in nature. Often the childrens' interest will be piqued, and they will study a topic intensely for weeks afterwards. For example, we launched a study of medieval times after watching "Camelot." After viewing the mini-series, "Roots," Ginny delved deeply into the history of slavery in America, and did a term paper on the Underground Railroad.

Some years we have focused on one particular area for the study of geography. One year we decided to become experts on Europe. During that period, we read such books as **Heidi**, **Lassie Come Home**, **A Tale of Two Cities**, **Oliver Twist**, **The Hiding Place**, and **Anne Frank: The Diary of a Young Girl.** We also watched a few movies that were based in Europe, including **The Sound of Music**, and **Night Crossing**, which dealt with an escape from East Germany. As we read these books, we took out the maps and the globe and followed the action closely. We also witnessed a reenactment of the Japanese attack on Pearl Harbor. That experience, coupled with the reading we were doing, led to a related study of World War II.

Another year, we decided to focus on the Middle East. Among other things, we made an Egyptian meal, studied hieroglyphics, and learned about the pyramids. We coupled this topic with Bible study in the Old Testament, where we charted the wanderings of the Israelites in the wilderness, and learned about the "old names" for such lands as modern-day Iran and Iraq.

Some people refer to this type of learning as the "unit study approach." However, we do things a little differently from most people who believe in unit studies. For one thing, most of the projects are conceived, planned, and executed by the children. My main role is usually to devise a general plan of action and start reading a good book to them or come up with an appropriate video. Almost always, a couple of the children become motivated to study the topic on their own. Then, their enthusiasm helps get the rest involved, even if they just wind up listening to the "interested parties" expound on what they are learning about the subject. If no one happens to find a particular topic interesting, we usually drop the matter and go on to something else. In most cases, the exact same item will come up again at a later date and will "click" with somebody the second time around.

We also tend to emphasize the literary aspects of these experiences, rather than the "active learning" component. Most advocates of "unit studies" do vast quantities of "activities," but we prefer a more "laid-back" approach. My children might play with "knight costumes" made from garbage can lids and cardboard after listening to "Ivanhoe," or watching "Robin Hood," but that is different from having "Mom" plan a unit on medieval times, and incorporate a day of "costume making" to be followed by a "culminating activity" like a medieval feast. I'm not saying there is anything wrong with that approach if your whole family enjoys it. It just doesn't suit us!

If you do choose to use unit studies, it helps to have a time line on the wall someplace. That way the children will gradually get a feel for the overall flow of history. As they study various events or time periods, they can fill in items on the time line. I have found the time line means more to them if it also includes whatever family history you know. Now that they realize that their great-grandfather was born right after the Civil War, and that their grandfather was unemployed during the Great Depression and stationed in England during World War II, my children have a better feel for when these events actually took place.

At our house, subjects like economics and political science are mainly learned through discussion. As soon as the children are old enough to understand, we begin trying to bring them into discussions about current events and the state of the economy. We all enjoy debating issues and getting involved in local politics. As usual, our use of textbooks in these areas is extremely limited, except when we use them to look up answers to specific questions.

The Fine Arts

We tend to be a very "artsy" family, so incorporating learning experiences in dance, art, drama, and music has come easily to us. We try to broaden our experiences by learning to appreciate a variety of art forms, and limit our actual participation to those which we enjoy as individuals. Ginny enjoys jazz and tap dancing in addition to the theatre. Sam is a talented musician, and so is my husband, Roy. Dan is following in Sam's musical footsteps and is also a budding cartoonist. Laura practically lives for art. I have always enjoyed puttering around in a number of art forms, but I've never achieved true expertise in any of them.

In families that don't have natural tendencies towards the arts, the best approach to stimulate interest may be to set up art or music centers and try to make them appear inviting. We keep many different materials in our art center.   In addition to the typical paints, brushes, markers, and crayons, there is a wide variety of boxes, styrofoam meat trays, old paper towel tubes, bits of yarn, collage materials, etc. This is all stored inside a counter, easily accessible to everyone. (Unfortunately, it is also accessible to our three-year-old, but that's another story...one that requires a great deal of patience and a lot of clean up time.) On top of the counter, we keep a variety of art books, such as books about artists, and "how to draw" books. We also have a box with reproductions of famous paintings. On a nearby wall there is plenty of room for budding artists to display their creations.

We also have a "music center." We own several "real" instruments, including an upright bass, a banjo, a mandolin, a violin, a piano, a baritone ukelele, an accordion and about twenty-five guitars! As soon as the children are capable of understanding that these are not toys and must be handled with care, we allow them to use these instruments anytime they want. We also have a tape player, and many tapes, including several sets of "classical" masterpieces. On a shelf nearby, there are several music-related games and activities, including "The Game of Great Composers." (I don't think anyone in our family has ever played it, though. They must not have, because the box is still intact. As I pointed out before, they often tend to ignore those items that look a little too "educational.")

Whenever we have a chance, we go to "cultural experiences," like plays and concerts, and also to experiences that aren't quite as cultural, like "old-timey fiddle contests" and bluegrass festivals. Once in awhile, we attend art exhibits, in order to provide Laura with experiences she might enjoy. Frankly, I could live without them, but it's fascinating to watch her interest develop, and see the new directions her art takes afterwards.

In Conclusion

The living curriculum that I have outlined often appeals to people with younger children. However, many people feel the need to go back to a more structured, subject-oriented approach when their children reach high school. I have fought this tendency myself. Round one occurred when Sam reached middle school age, and round two hit when he made it into ninth grade. Both times, we made a brief foray into the world of lesson plans and textbooks, and quickly decided to set them aside again. Not all students need to change their approach to learning just because they move over some invisible boundary line. By the time they are in high school, a lot depends on their individual interests, talents, and goals for the future. In the next chapter, we will consider the subject of the transition from childhood to adulthood, and see if we can find a way to make the move a bit less jolting for everyone concerned.

Chapter VI
On to Broadway!

At some point, every aspiring actor or actress starts dreaming of being a star on Broadway or the silver screen. Recently, we have had several conversations at our house in an attempt to gently dissuade Ginny from taking this course. I'm sure she will eventually take a different turn, and possibly try to coordinate a career as a high school drama coach with her desire to raise a family of her own someday. Perhaps she will maintain her interest in drama primarily as a hobby. Although I'd never try to actually stand in her way, I certainly hope she won't really try to fit in with the Broadway crowd.

During the early teenage years, it is natural for students to gradually try to define their own goals for their lives and their careers. Because many home schoolers have had the freedom to consider and pursue their own goals at an early age, some of them already know what they want to do by this time. For those who have not yet developed clear-cut interests or specific goals for the future, this is the time to help them locate opportunities to "try on" a variety of careers for size.

The best way to accomplish this is often through volunteer work in the community. This could be something typical, like participation in a "community service project" that has already been set up for teenagers, or it could require some serious legwork on your part. If students are interested in specific trades, you may have to help them search for adults who are willing to take them on as volunteers or apprentices for short trial periods.

Our children have done volunteer work at the library for several years. Ginny assists with programs for young children and helps out with book repair, and Sam shelves books, cleans up in the evenings, and is the resident "paper cutter" for the crafts department. Ginny's work with the preschoolers, coupled with an occasional babysitting stint, has helped her recognize her own natural talent for working with youngsters. She has also found out that she is a "people person" who is most happy when she has others to work with. Sam, on the other hand, has always been a bit of a loner. He has confirmed that he prefers working on his own and immersing himself in his music. Although he is friendly and outgoing, he doesn't share Ginny's need to be constantly surrounded by people.

Teenagers in America

The entire view of "teenagers" in modern America is a very artificial construct. In most older societies, when the young people reached puberty, they began to take on adult roles. Even in early America, the teenagers spent most of their time actively preparing for specific occupations. The girls were primarily instructed in the art of homemaking, and the boys often were apprenticed to master craftsmen. Very few were actually required to continue academic preparation past the elementary years. Those that remained in school through the upper levels were destined for lives as ministers, scholars, statesmen, or merchants, and recognized that they, too, were preparing for clearly-defined futures.

Many home-schooling mothers complain because their formerly well-behaved twelve or thirteen-year-old sons suddenly become sullen or rebellious and begin to balk at the academic work that came easily to them in the early grades. This is *not* an automatic feature of puberty. It is a direct result of the artificial set-up in American society that attempts to keep adolescent boys as "children" long after their bodies are telling them that they are turning into adults.

These young men are only feeling the urge to begin moving towards their adult roles! If they are still treated like schoolboys and required to sit for long periods of time doing nothing but assigned academic work, it is only natural that they will begin to rebel. This may be especially true with home-schooling adolescents who are kept at home for most of the day surrounded by a pack of younger siblings.

Similarly, girls at this age are likely to begin focusing on one specific part of their adult role: the search for a mate! That is the reason for all the sudden "silliness," and the focus on clothes and personal appearance that characterizes so many adolescent girls in today's society. If these young ladies do not begin to clarify their own goals and make specific progress towards them, they may start to look towards a peer group for social gratification and gradually turn away from their families.

Preparing for the Future

By the time students reach high school age, it is even more important to treat them as individuals. Some plan to attend college. They will need to prepare for entrance tests and keep sufficient records to prove that they have taken certain required high school courses. Some may want to earn actual diplomas and will decide to go with structured programs or correspondence courses. Others may be interested in locating appropriate apprenticeships or earning their G.E.D.s early. They may desire to take community college courses or move directly into the world of work. It is crucial that the students themselves make these plans, rather than their parents. Unless the teens have had significant input into the planning phase, they will generally be recalcitrant when it comes to putting forth the required effort.

Sam is our oldest son. Next summer, at the age of sixteen, he is planning on taking the G.E.D. He wants to work in the music business eventually. If he was fixated on becoming a "star," I'd probably be a little concerned, but his plans are much broader. He has already been performing in public, and has two years experience teaching guitar. In addition, he has built several instruments on his own. At this point, he is considering taking some electronics courses at the community college to learn more about the construction of electronic instruments and is also looking into the possibility of an apprenticeship at several local music stores. He is most interested in the repair business, but is also considering opening up his own store someday. Of course, in the back of his mind is the hope that he may be able to earn a living as a performer, either as a "headliner" or a "studio musician."

There are several reasons I like Sam's plan. First of all, it is based on a solid interest which has developed over

the course of several years. It is not based on a sudden
"whim." He has already demonstrated the willingness to
commit many hours to practicing music and has successfully
completed several related projects. Second, although he has
definitely decided on a general course of action, he has the
sense to leave his options slightly open. He recognizes that
there is much for him to learn, and he is willing to do
whatever it takes to reach his goal. If this should include
college at some point, I'm confident he will be able to handle
that, too. Right now, it is not something that he plans to do.
If he decides to go back later, as an adult student, it will not
be as necessary to substantiate his high school coursework.
He can always take the S.A.T. later if necessary, or attend a
community college for a year in order to demonstrate his
ability before applying to a major university.

Ginny, on the other hand, says she definitely wants to
go to college right after high school, in order to major in
drama. If that is the case, she will probably want to finish
the twelfth grade and keep detailed records of the subjects
she is taking. There has even been some talk of her going to
"real high school" next year to participate in the drama
program. At this point, we haven't decided if that will be an
option or not. Whenever we do make our decision, it will be
based on a careful assessment of the entire situation, taking
into account her individual needs and maturity level. She

won't be stopped just because "we are a home-schooling family," or because I happen to write books about the subject! I'm still hoping we will be able to find enough additional sources of drama participation to meet her needs without returning to the public school arena. We may also look for a school district that will allow part-time enrollment or will welcome her into the drama program as an extra-curricular event.

The Academic Scene

Obviously, I don't believe that students automatically have to go back to a formal, subject-centered approach, using textbooks and structured assignments, just because they reach a certain age. However, those students who wish to prepare for college may be asked to substantiate their high school "credits" for an admissions officer some day. In the last chapter, we are going to deal with record keeping and address this issue in some detail.

Other than an increased need for record-keeping and dividing the curriculum up into subject areas for reporting purposes, learning experiences do not need to "mutate" just because students are getting older. As in the elementary grades, I have learned to focus primarily on long-range goals during the high school years. The main difference is that the students' own goals have begun to shape up, and assume a high priority. That doesn't mean that I "forget" the goals I have set. We just have to work harder at cooperation, in order to ensure that we remain on the same wavelength.

Preparing for College

As a former college teacher, I know a little about what is necessary for success in the university environment. The most important requirement is that students can read and write fluently. This refers not only to their ability, but their speed. At the college level, students are asked to read large quantities of material on a strict time schedule and must be able to write essay questions within prescribed time limits.

Students will find it helpful to have developed skills in typing, using a computer, taking notes, and making outlines. Some of these peripheral skills can be developed through a "crash course" just before college. There are excellent materials available to help students learn skills like note-taking and how to adjust reading speeds to a variety of materials.

Other, more subtle skills, are also necessary. Students need to learn how to play "university games," such as "scoping out" teachers to figure out what kinds of exams they give. They must be able to rapidly assess who will lean heavily on lecture material and who will test from the book. They have to be able to lay out a schedule based on information from previous students. They don't want to get three professors who are all sticklers for long, library-researched term papers in the same semester!

Of course, some of these skills can't really be learned until the students get to college. However, it may help if they can take a few community college courses for "practice" during high school, or if they can arrange to visit a number of university classes. The best preparation they can have, however, is to be excellent communicators, with well-developed skills in the areas of listening, speaking, reading and writing.

In order to get to college in the first place, students also have to learn the art of test taking. In our family, we never believed in testing, but we often "played" with tests, just to learn something about them. We made up matching exercises and discussed how to "get into the teacher's mindset" when choosing the answers to multiple-choice questions. When preparing for the G.E.D., we had Sam write several essays on "surprise subjects" within a 45-minute time limit.

One of the difficulties home-schooled students often face is the necessity of doing things quickly when they are being timed. Our first experience with this was on a standardized test when Sam was in the second grade. He scored in the ninetieth-percentile range on all subjects except math computation. I couldn't figure out why, when he understood the subject so well, until the next year when I gave him a similar test myself. There were two students in the room, a friend of ours and Sam. The friend had previous experience in the school system. He sat and worked diligently on the test, using one finger to keep his place on the answer sheet, while the other hand moved down the question page. Sam sat on the other side, doodling and staring off into the distance. Every time he looked at the question sheet, he lost his place on the answer pad. Naturally, he did poorly on the math computation section again, despite the fact that he got every problem correct that he actually completed. That experience taught me the necessity for "practicing" such test-taking behaviors, and throwing in occasional timed drills, especially in math.

One other thing I have done to prepare Sam and Ginny for college was teach them how to research and write term papers. Many professors automatically assume that students already know how to do this when they get to college. We took out a college reference manual, and I showed them how to make note cards and bibliography cards, and then we spent some time at the library learning about computer searches and how to use the "Reader's Guide to

Periodicals." They were allowed to choose their own subjects, but we worked together to make sure that the subjects were neither too broad nor too limited for a ten-page paper.

Another area requiring some preparation is the development of oral communication skills. When it comes time to listen to lectures, I'm sure all of our oral reading experiences will come in handy. (I just hope they have teachers who aren't too boring!) Although neither Sam nor Ginny are accomplished orators, they have had experience with speaking before groups. Ginny has served as president of her 4-H group, and Sam has considerable stage experience as a performer. He has also given several speeches as a 4-H'er, explaining guitar construction or related subjects.

In Conclusion

If you respect your teens, demonstrate that you value them as individuals, solicit their input in the planning process, grant them the freedom to make their own mistakes, and help them move out gradually into the surrounding community, I'm sure you will get through this period with a minimum of scars. In our family, responsibilities and privileges are treated as two sides of the same coin. The more the teenagers act like responsible adults, the more we loosen the old apron strings and grant them their independence. At this point, everything is working quite well. Of course, we still have a long way to go. Perhaps I shouldn't even be writing this chapter yet! I'll come back in a few years and give you an update. Then you can decide whether or not you should have been listening to me!

Chapter VII
Answering the Critics

On the morning after opening night, the actors and actresses hold their breath collectively as they wait for the first reviews of the play to appear in the newspaper. As homeschoolers, we must also face occasional reviews. Thankfully, we usually have a little more control over the process than they do in the theatre.

Some lucky home-schooling parents have no legal requirements to face such reviews. For the first six years, we lived in a state that left us completely alone. For the past several years, however, I have had to learn how to add structure "after the fact," in order to appease those authorities who have a hard time understanding our approach to education.

When facing one of these reviews, I always try to take the lead myself, rather than allowing the other party to direct the course of the interview. If I give them the opportunity to ask the questions, I have found it is easy to wind up having trouble giving answers they consider are "appropriate." The best way to assume such control over the interview is to be well-prepared.

Although it's important that you understand your own "philosophy of education" so you can defend your ideas if challenged, it is not always the best idea to start off an interview by explaining how your beliefs about learning differ from those of the authorities. One of my friends was in the middle of such an interview earlier this year. Just as it was coming to a successful conclusion, her husband, who had recently attended one of my workshops, walked in and proceeded to lay out their entire philosophy of education. The next day the supervisor showed up at their door with an armful of basal readers, and said, "This is what you're supposed to be doing in first grade!"

Generally, I come to these interviews armed with several items. To begin with, I always have a list of the reading that the children have been doing. I refer to this as a "sample" of their reading, even if I have listed every single book they happened to look at that year. I also bring along a few examples of their current math and writing. Then I write out a narrative that explains what we have been doing in the areas of science, social studies, fine arts, and physical education, which are all required subject areas in our state.

In Pennsylvania, where I serve as an evaluator, the home educators are also required to prepare both a "portfolio" and a "log." Their portfolios are similar to scrapbooks. Their superintendents are looking for "sustained" progress in each subject area. Therefore, the parents are expected to include several samples of work in math and writing, and to choose some from the beginning, the middle, and the end of the year. Naturally, if they need to demonstrate such progress, they must make sure that the papers from the end of the year look better than the ones from the beginning of the year!

Although our state does not require a log, I keep one anyway on my computer. I'm not very good about writing down everything that we do on a daily basis, but I try to jot down something at least once a week. A typical entry might read, "Today we went to the science museum and discussed the exhibit on the Chesapeake Bay," or "Today we went into the garden, discussed how worms aerate the ground, and planted tomato seedlings." A social studies note might read, "Ginny just watched the mini-series, *Roots*, and went to the library to find information on Harriet Tubman," or "Today we went to the battlefield at Gettysburg, took a tour of the grounds, and brought home a book on the Civil War that we purchased at the bookstore." (There are also days, of course, when the entry would have to say, "Today we laid around in our pajamas, made some popcorn, and watched a video with no educational value whatsoever." Generally, I don't mention those days when making my log.)

Just before the reviewer is due to visit, I print out this computerized log and put labels in the margins to indicate the subject areas covered. In other words, I jot down "science" next to the note on the science museum, and "social studies" next to the comment about Harriet Tubman. Then I look over all those comments, and write a couple of paragraphs about each separate subject area. (Because it is not required, I don't show the supervisors the log itself.)

Sometimes, when I become very busy, I forget to keep my log. When that happens, I find out just how important it is! I run from room to room, asking the kids, "Quick! Help me out, here! What did we do in social studies this year!" Needless to say, this approach does not work very well.

Whether or not your state requires them, it is also impressive to have a list of some of your "goals" for the year written down to show the reviewer. If you take this approach, be prepared to discuss how well those goals were met. In states where portfolios are required, people sometimes use a notebook with dividers between each subject area. On the dividers, they write down a few goals for that subject, and then include samples of work, pictures from field trips, etc.

I'm glad our state doesn't ask for such involved portfolios, but some people actually seem to enjoy putting them together. You might even impress yourself with how much you managed to do in a single year!

Record-Keeping for High School Students

For those high school students who live in states with "laid-back laws," there may be no reason to keep more structured records, especially if the students are not planning to try to get an actual diploma. However, if your students desire a diploma or have definite plans to go on to college right after high school, or if your school district requires certain "credits" for the high school years, it may be necessary to formalize your record-keeping procedures.

This does not mean you necessarily have to move back to a textbook approach, unless you want to. For example, if my son was supposed to be taking "biology" in ninth grade, I might need to substantiate that he had undergone a certain number of hours of instruction and studied biology-related concepts. However, due to legal precedents established many years ago, the officials have no right to insist that we use a particular approach.

Suppose Sam went down to the stream, and brought home some tadpoles to raise in a bowl. He might have cut up fish to see what they ate, or raised tomato plants from seeds. Any of these experiences would be considered "biology." He might also have read interesting books on related subjects from the library, gone to a museum and written a report about the experience, or visited a marine lab for a week and volunteered his services. In order to have such experiences count, I would need to keep scrupulous records of the actual hours he spent doing such activities, and make sure they eventually added up to the required hours. I would also need to keep some kind of "proof," such as reports, pictures, postcards, projects, or exhibits. Some people refer to this approach to record-keeping as "portfolio management." I sometimes call it the "shoe-box method." That probably gives you an indication of how organized my own records tend to be. However, as I pointed out earlier, Sam has no desire to actually get a diploma, and won't be going right on to college. It hasn't been as important to maintain strict records for him as it will be for Ginny next year.

For students who plan to go to college, it is probably important to have a variety of standardized test scores in their portfolios, particularly the PSAT and SAT or ACT. The PSAT is usually given in the tenth grade, and may be a valuable source of scholarships for people who score high.

In addition to test scores and records of individual classes, it is also helpful to begin gathering a "resume" for each student, which lists volunteer work, paid work experiences, and other community involvements, such as membership in church groups, scouts, or 4-H. Begin asking people to write "To Whom It May Concern" recommendation letters early. Sometimes it is difficult to track people down later, when such letters may be needed. If your children have been volunteering at the library, or have a good relationship with a particular scout leader, don't hesitate to ask them for their assistance in this matter.

In Conclusion

When it comes time for any of our children to enter college, I have no worries at all about "answering the critics," despite our relaxed approach to education. As a former university teacher, I have seen the appalling communication skills of the typical students in our teacher preparation program. During my brief career, it seemed like I spent half my time trying to explain the difference between complete sentences and phrases, and the other half trying to talk the students into coming up to the front and giving presentations without passing out. If my children have good communication skills and are capable of writing essays explaining their goals and why they want to attend a particular college, I know that they will be accepted with open arms. If they can add in a few good test scores and a handful of letters of recommendation, I'll be surprised if the admission officers don't beg them to attend. If, in addition to all that, they have prepared a portfolio that lists credit hours earned, and contains proof of a variety of unique learning experiences, the admissions officers may just hyperventilate and keel over.

Whatever the future holds for my children, our main purposes for them will have been achieved if they grow up to be mature individuals, who have adopted our family's value system, developed their own talents, and prepared themselves for earning a living doing something that will bring them satisfaction. These have been the main goals that have guided our efforts so far. Whatever your own goals are for your family, I feel confident that you will be able to achieve them, too. Although we all need to try to meet our "critics" halfway, and answer their questions as best as we can, they are not the parties to whom we owe our ultimate responsibility or allegiance.

Although I'm constantly trying to fight a tendency towards excessive "pride," I must say that I am proud of our children, proud of the job my husband and I have done so far, and proud of the fact that we dared to take control over our children's education. If you assume similar control, you will undoubtedly feel that same sense of satisfaction someday. I hope this book has helped you gain the confidence to begin or continue in your own home-schooling efforts. If you have any comments, or want to tell me how you are doing, I'd love to hear from you. Write me at the address in the back of the book! I can't promise to answer everyone promptly, but I'll try my best! I've also started writing a short newsletter from time to time, and will be happy to send you a complimentary subscription if you are interested.

Postscript: No O.B.E. for me!

While I was wrapping up the first draft of this book, I went to a discussion in Pennsylvania about the new "outcomes-based education" that is being jammed down the throats of local school systems there. They passed out a booklet that discussed several proposed changes to the curriculum. As I read it, I noticed that they were advocating several of the same suggestions I have included in this book, such as integrated curricula, portfolios, and a decreased reliance on grades.

I'm as opposed to "outcomes-based education" as anyone on this planet, but I'm afraid that some of the people who are fighting this issue are confusing the "goals" of the O.B.E. proponents with their methods. That's like complaining that "lectures" will corrupt our young people, or that "editing stories" is an evil process. The processes of integrating a curriculum, or devising alternate forms of evaluations, are things that can be done by people with many different agendas.

The important items to focus on when fighting O.B.E., (or supporting it if you happen to be on the other side of the fence), are the *goals* that are being developed for the schools. The methods that are going to be used are secondary. As you can see from the material in this book, I personally believe that some of the methods they are proposing are actually superior to the processes of lecturing and testing, memorizing and forgetting, that have characterized schools for many years. That's what scares me! This time, when they put forth goals like standardizing children and teaching relative morality, they might just succeed! (Naturally, these are not the goals that they mention in the literature. You have to read between the lines.) If you care about traditional values, you'd better start educating yourself about this issue, because it is going to be one of the biggest fights that we have ever witnessed in the educational arena, and the stakes are high. But please, don't ever call me an "outcomes advocate" just because I believe in the importance of goals, and happen to use some of the same methods as the people on the other side! Look back at my goals, and focus on them, instead!

For a FREE subscription to the newsletter

"The Relaxed Home Schooler"

Write to:

Mary Hood

Ambleside Educational Press

P.O. Box 2524
Cartersville, GA 30120